D1243243

The Library of the Nine Planets™

NEPTUNE

Chris Hayhurst

rosen central™

The Rosen Publishing Group, Inc., New York

Published in 2005 by The Rosen Publishing Group, Inc.
29 East 21st Street, New York, NY 10010

Library of Congress Cataloging-in-Publication Data

Hayhurst, Chris.
Neptune/by Chris Hayhurst.
      p. cm.—(The library of the nine planets)
Summary: Presents scientific discoveries about the atmosphere, composition, size, moons, and strange weather systems of this outer planet known as a gaseous giant.
Includes bibliographical references and index.
ISBN 1-4042-0171-8 (library binding)
1. Neptune (Planet)—Juvenile literature. [1. Neptune (Planet)]
I. Title. II. Series.
QB691.H39 2004
523.48'1—dc22

2003022409

Manufactured in the United States of America

On the cover: An image of Neptune taken by *Voyager 2.*

Contents

ONE

TWO

THREE

FOUR

Introduction   5

An Unlikely Discovery   7

The Interesting Features of Neptune   18

Neptune's Violent Weather   29

The Present and the Future   36

Timeline of Exploration and Discovery   39

Glossary   40

For More Information   42

For Further Reading   44

Bibliography   45

Index   46

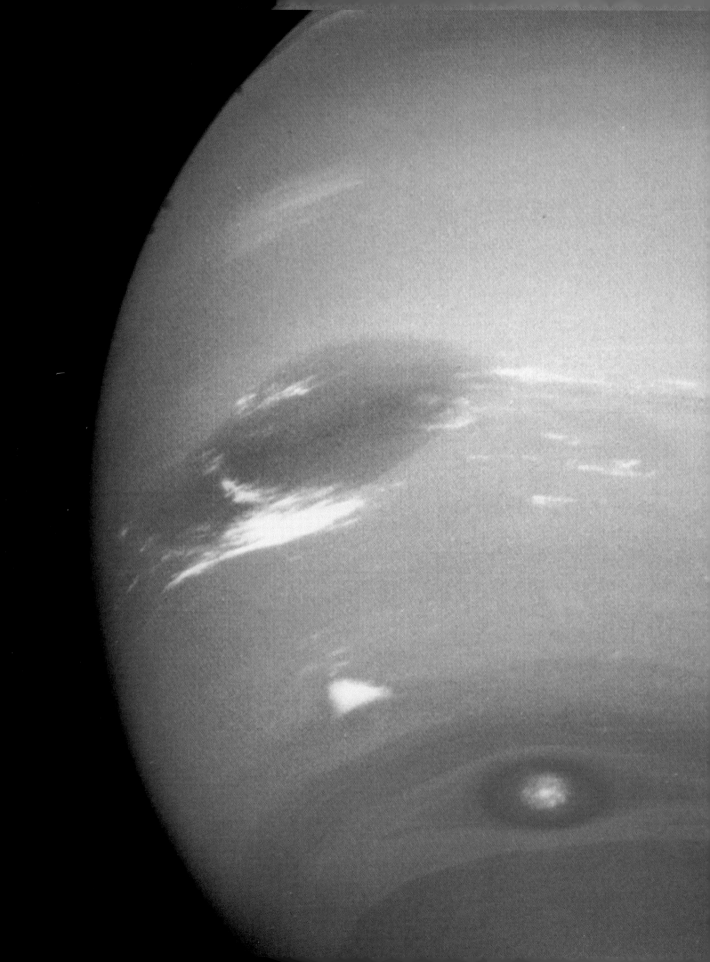

INTRODUCTION

If you've ever dreamed of becoming an astronaut or even if you've just looked up at the night sky, you might have wondered what it's like in space. How does it feel to be weightless? Is space hot or cold or somewhere in between? What's out there?

People have struggled with this last question for thousands of years. Even the caveman must have stared up at the darkness late at night and wondered what he was seeing. He saw millions of white dots from horizon to horizon; the massive Moon floating slowly across the sky; and the vast black blanket that held it all together. A few hours later, he saw the bright, hot Sun, which, when it rose, signaled the start of another day.

For the last several hundred years, astronomers have devoted their lives to studying space. They've trained their telescopes toward the night sky and drawn maps of what they've seen. They've marked and named nearly every speck of light they've discovered, distinguishing stars from planets, moons, asteroids, and comets. They've explored the solar system by observing from Earth, then launched spaceships into the sky to take a closer look.

Every year, even today, they make new discoveries. In March 2004, for example, scientists announced the discovery of the "planetoid" Sedna, orbiting beyond Pluto. Space is full of undiscovered wonders, and the many mysteries of the solar system are just waiting to be unraveled. In fact, it may just be up to you, future astronomers, astronauts, and space buffs, to unravel those secrets. What will we learn next?

Picture this: It's the year 2030. You're the top astronaut at NASA, the one all the others look up to. You've had years of experience in space—trips to the Moon, a short jaunt to Mars, months spent conducting scientific experiments aboard the International Space Station. And now you've been handed an assignment like no other: You've been sent to study the planet Neptune.

No one has ever been to Neptune before. Sure, it's been studied, and astronomers have learned a lot about the eighth most distant planet from the Sun since it was first discovered more than 200 years ago. They know it is gigantic—more than seventeen times as heavy as Earth and nearly four times as large, measured from pole to pole.

They know a little about its atmosphere, like the fact that it's mainly made of the gases hydrogen, helium, and methane. And they know a few things about its many moons and its strange weather systems. But this trip—the one you're on right this moment—could potentially help scientists learn more about Neptune than ever before. After all, what could be better than actually going to the planet in person, to see it for yourself?

This mission you're on is huge, nearly as big as your destination. What you learn could change the way the world looks at space. What you find could make history.

An Unlikely Discovery

Neptune has been around for a long, long time—billions of years, in fact. This is far longer than humans have lived on Earth. But it wasn't until the early 1800s, just about 200 years ago, that people realized this planet existed at all. You see, Neptune is extremely far away, more than 2.5 billion miles (4 billion kilometers) from Earth. You can't see Neptune from Earth with the naked eye. So for millions of years, people had no idea Neptune was even part of our solar system. They had no idea there even was a Neptune.

Alexis Bouvard

Around 1820, however, that changed. A man named Alexis Bouvard, who worked as an astronomer in France, was busy studying the planet Uranus. Up until that point, Uranus was the farthest known planet from the Sun. Most astronomers believed Uranus was it, the seventh and last planet in our solar system. But as Bouvard, a relatively unknown assistant to the well-respected French astronomer Pierre-Simon Laplace, studied his data, he wasn't so sure.

Bouvard's job was to map out the entire orbit of Uranus. An orbit is the path a planet takes as it travels around the Sun. His goal was to make a precise chart showing exactly where Uranus should be in space at all times. It was a well-known fact that planets orbit the Sun in regular patterns

Asteroids
Jupiter
Saturn
Uranus
Neptune

Sun
Mercury
Venus
Earth
Mars

This computer illustration shows the relative sizes of the planets' orbits. The orbits of Mercury, Venus, Earth, and Mars are magnified, which shows how small the orbits are compared to those of the outer planets. The distance between the Earth and the Sun is 1 astronomical unit (AU). To give a sense of the size of Neptune's orbit, the distance between it and Uranus alone is 10 AU.

according to the laws of physics. It would therefore be possible for Bouvard to use mathematical equations to predict Uranus's location in the universe at any point in the future.

Bouvard got to work. He gathered the data. He crunched the numbers. And then he discovered something very disturbing. His calculations, which he took extreme care to ensure were correct, showed Uranus's orbit was slightly different than what was predicted based on visual observations from Earth. For some reason, past observations made by astronomers using telescopes from Earth did not match his mathematical calculations. In other words, while everyone else believed Uranus's orbit should send it in one direction, his math put it in a completely different direction. He could have made a mistake, but that was unlikely. Bouvard knew his numbers. Something was up. Things just didn't make sense.

Bouvard thought about the discrepancy for some time. And then he had an idea. Perhaps, he thought, Uranus's orbit was being thrown out of whack by something else in space. It was a well-known fact, for example, that Earth's orbit was influenced by the Moon. The Moon is so large that it actually pulls Earth toward it by a force called gravity. Maybe there was something in space close enough that its gravity would change the orbit of Uranus. Maybe there was a celestial body in space that had yet to be discovered.

As word got out about Bouvard's findings, well-known astronomers around the world began to theorize about what could be causing Uranus's strange orbit. Some believed a comet had slammed into the planet in the years since the old observations were made. They thought such a hit could have permanently altered the planet's path. But others, including Bouvard, thought an explanation like that was highly unlikely. There was no way a tiny comet hitting such a large planet could have an effect like the one he had observed. It would take something far bigger than that.

Other astronomers began to question the laws of physics. Perhaps everything was different that far out in space. Maybe the equations and theories used to explain the way things move and behave on Earth didn't apply to Uranus. If that were the case, it would be no wonder that Bouvard's calculations put Uranus on an orbit different than that observed from Earth.

Urbain-Jean-Joseph LeVerrier

The first astronomer to suggest publicly that there may be another planet distant to Uranus that had yet to be discovered was a French

Urbain-Jean-Joseph LeVerrier, shown here, first predicted the existence of Neptune. LeVerrier, however, is not considered to have been the sole discoverer of the planet. It was also pinpointed at the same time, independently, by John Couch Adams.

mathematician and astronomer named Urbain-Jean-Joseph LeVerrier. LeVerrier worked at the Paris Observatory, a respected center for space research at the time. Like Bouvard, LeVerrier was an excellent mathematician in addition to being a great astronomer. He put pencil to paper and began doing the math. He thought if he calculated the numbers just right he might be able to predict exactly where this missing planet could be found. Then all he would have to do would be to point his telescope to the right spot.

Other astronomers listened to LeVerrier and began to think he was on to something. They read his papers explaining his theory and looked over his calculations. Soon astronomers around the world were using LeVerrier's work to narrow their own searches for the yet-to-be-discovered planet. It was only a matter time before they had a breakthrough.

The Discovery

Then, finally, in the fall of 1846, the breakthrough came. On September 23, a German by the name of Johann Gottfried Galle, an employee of the Berlin Observatory, found the planet with his telescope. The massive object, although it looked the size of a pinprick through his lens, was almost exactly where LeVerrier had said it should be. Neptune had been discovered. Astronomers could add one more planet to their maps of the solar system.

Today Urbain-Jean-Joseph LeVerrier gets most of the credit for calculating Neptune's precise location. But although LeVerrier certainly did determine the planet's whereabouts and should be honored for his work, he wasn't the only one to do so. In fact, at the same time LeVerrier published his predictions, another astronomer, named John Couch Adams, was also hard at work to find the missing planet.

Adams, from England, put the planet in almost the exact same spot and might have done so slightly earlier than LeVerrier. Unfortunately for Adams, however, his work was not published as quickly and therefore did not receive the recognition that LeVerrier's calculations did. Astronomers and politicians from England and France argued for years over who should be honored for the true theoretical discovery, and ultimately it was agreed that both men should be recognized for their accomplishments.

The Planet Mistaken for a Star

Although Neptune was officially discovered in 1846, that wasn't the first time it was seen. More than two centuries earlier, in 1613, the famous Italian astronomer and physicist Galilei Galileo observed the planet high up in the night sky, a wink of light amid millions of others. To Galileo, however, the planet looked like a star, and that's what he decided it was. If he had investigated further and if he had had a telescope powerful enough to do so, what we know as Neptune today might have been called Galileo.

Along with Urbain-Jean-Joseph LeVerrier, John Couch Adams, shown here, is often credited with discovering Neptune. Adams calculated that the planet existed in the same spot as LeVerrier did.

The Voyager Missions

In 1977, engineers at the National Aeronautics and Space Administration (NASA) launched a spacecraft into the sky. It was scheduled to visit Jupiter, Saturn, Uranus, and Neptune. The news took many people by surprise. How could they possibly send a spaceship that far into space? Could a human-made craft even survive such a long journey so deep into the solar system?

Despite the lingering doubts, however, the mission was clear. Two spacecraft called Voyager were launched within weeks of each other. *Voyager 2* took off on August 20, 1977. *Voyager 1*, so named because it would reach the planets earlier than *Voyager 2* even though it was launched later, was blasted into the sky on September 5, 1977.

As the two spacecraft raced into the darkness of the solar system, their paths took them in slightly different directions. But this was exactly what NASA engineers wanted. *Voyager 2* was designed to explore Jupiter and Saturn, and then continue on to Uranus and Neptune. *Voyager 1* would go as far as Jupiter and Saturn, but then its mission would be over. The deepest solar system exploration would be up to its twin sister.

Voyager 2 arrived at Jupiter in July 1979, four months after *Voyager 1*. Following the directions of preprogrammed computers on

Voyager 2 lifted off on August 20, 1977, sixteen days before *Voyager 1*. It was launched aboard the Titan Centaur rocket, shown here. Though *Voyager 2* was launched first, it arrived at its first destination, Jupiter, several months later than *Voyager 1*. It would eventually travel on alone to Neptune and provide scientists with a wealth of data about the planet.

board, the ships used high-tech cameras to take pictures of the planets. They also took samples of the planets' atmospheres. They didn't have long to do their work, however, as they continued to hurtle through space, quickly leaving the planet behind. Next stop: Saturn.

Between planets, *Voyager 1* and *Voyager 2* didn't just take time off. They continued to work hard, collecting data on the interplanetary space they traveled through. As the information accumulated, it was sent by computer back to Earth, where scientists at NASA could analyze it. It was the first time ever that data from deep space could be looked at so closely.

Voyager 1 reached Saturn in November 1980. *Voyager 2*, now lagging quite far behind, arrived months later in August 1981. While near Saturn, the ships collected data similar to the information they gathered from Jupiter.

At this point it was time for the two craft to go their own ways, and *Voyager 2*, as planned, was sent off on its long trip to Uranus and Neptune. It would be almost five years before *Voyager 2* arrived at Uranus, then another three and a half years before it reached Neptune in August 1989. But the lengthy journey was well worth it.

Voyager 2 not only took photographs of Neptune, but it discovered six new satellites orbiting the enormous planet. These satellites were in fact moons, like the Moon that orbits Earth. It also found that Triton possessed geological formations called geysers very similar to those found on Earth. The geysers were craters opening deep into Triton's surface and spewed gases into the atmosphere.

The images beamed back to Earth from Neptune also showed that Neptune had rings that completely circled the planet. This was intriguing to scientists because, even though they knew the rings existed, they thought they were broken and incomplete, sort of "ring arcs"

When a spacecraft is launched into space, we see, for the most part, the amazing photographs it takes as well as images of the craft itself. However, we rarely see the instruments that control that spacecraft and the scientists behind them. Shown here is the mission control room at NASA's Jet Propulsion Laboratory. This is where scientists controlled the spacecraft *Voyager 2*.

instead of true rings. The photographs and atmospheric data from *Voyager 2* showed the rings to be made of very fine dustlike material.

The Great Dark Spot

Another major discovery thanks to *Voyager 2* was that Neptune has incredibly stormy weather. Scientists had thought that Neptune was far too cold a place for storms to form. They believed the icy temperatures would prevent the atmosphere from creating massive weather systems. But the photographs proved otherwise. A massive dark area over Neptune's surface—an area bigger than Earth—stood

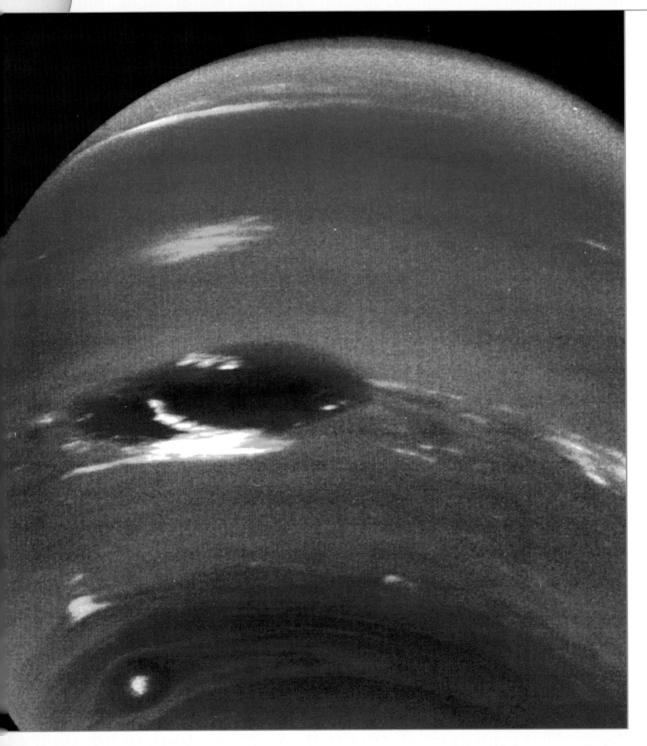

This image, taken by *Voyager 2*, shows Neptune's Great Dark Spot and the storm called Scooter (in the lower left corner, just above the dark spot with the white core). The winds, which blow at several hundred miles per hour, are pushing these storms eastward, or from right to left. Though the winds driving these storms around the planet are strong, the winds within the Great Dark Spot have been measured as some of the strongest known in the solar system.

out in almost all the pictures. This area was soon named the Great Dark Spot and was a huge storm. The Great Dark Spot could be seen in Neptune's southern hemisphere. But it wasn't just standing still. Incredible winds were blowing the spot toward the west. These winds moved the spot along at 700 miles per hour (1,127 km/h). It was like nothing ever seen before.

Other storm spots were also discovered. One, a small white cloud that motors completely around the planet every sixteen hours, is known affectionately to astronomers as Scooter. Even today, scientists aren't quite sure what sort of weather-related phenomenon Scooter is. It remains one of the many mysteries of space.

The Interesting Features of Neptune

Neptune is a complicated planet. Like Earth, it has an atmosphere made of a mix of gases. And also like Earth, it has weather systems and climate, storms and clouds, rocks and ice. But there are hundreds of other things scientists know about Neptune, and there are likely hundreds more yet to be discovered.

To help you get a grasp of just what makes Neptune unique, without getting bogged down in all the details, we've broken the planet down to its bare bones. The following features of Neptune were observed by space experts—the astronomers, astrophysicists, and other scientists who devote their lives to studying the solar system.

The Moons of Neptune

Yes, that's right, moons. Neptune is not like Earth. It isn't covered with deep blue oceans and green forests. Nothing lives on Neptune. And there isn't just one moon. Neptune has multiple moons—thirteen, in fact. There may even be more moons orbiting Neptune that have yet to be discovered. We'll just have to wait and see.

Years ago, astronomers were convinced that Neptune had just one moon like Earth. This moon, Triton, was discovered in 1846 by a scientist named William Lassell. Lassell, like John

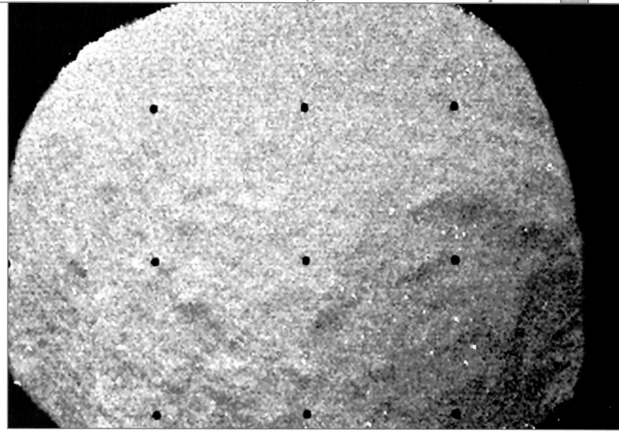

One of Neptune's thirteen moons, Proteus, shown here, is the largest next to Triton. This image of Proteus was taken by *Voyager 2* from a distance of 89,482 miles (144,000 km). Proteus measures about 199 miles (320 km) across, which is relatively small compared to Earth's moon. Since Neptune is so far away, small moons like Proteus are difficult to see. Because of this, scientists are continuing to discover new moons. This gives us the hope that there are more to be discovered.

Couch Adams, was from England. Lassell probably found Triton because Triton is by far Neptune's largest satellite. It's the biggest object in space that orbits Neptune.

So how big is Triton? Modern-day technology has allowed scientists to calculate its exact diameter (length from pole to pole) as 1,678 miles (2,700 km). That's about two-thirds the distance across the United States. It sounds big, but it's not particularly big compared to some other moons in the solar system. Take our moon for example. It's 2,160 miles (3,476 km) in diameter.

Neptune's moon Triton is the largest as far as scientists know. This image of Triton was taken on August 24, 1989, from 330,000 miles (530,000 km) away by *Voyager 2*. Faint surface details can be seen, such as its volcano-like geysers and its surface of nitrogen and methane ice. From these photos, Triton was deemed to be the most interesting of Neptune's moons.

Triton orbits Neptune, but that doesn't mean it's anywhere near the planet. Triton is so far away from Neptune, in fact, that it takes nearly six days (5.88 days to be exact) for it to make one full orbit. Astronomers have calculated the distance at 220,500 miles (354,860 km).

When *Voyager 2* cruised by Neptune back in 1989, it took photographs of the planet's moons, including Triton. Compared to the other moons, however, Triton was particularly intriguing. When scientists back on Earth examined the images, they noticed volcanolike formations on Triton's surface. They determined that these mountainous structures were so-called geysers,

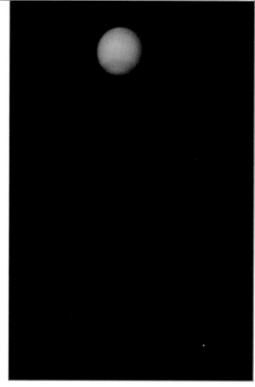

Triton is extremely far away from Neptune, as well as being much smaller than the planet. This image, taken by *Voyager 2*, shows Triton's size and distance relative to Neptune. Neptune is at the top. Triton is at the lower right.

which act like windows into the moon's insides and spit and spew nitrogen gas miles into the atmosphere. Thanks to all that nitrogen gas and a surface of nitrogen and methane ice, Triton has a pinkish color. The moon is also extremely cold. Estimates of its temperature

Dark Days

If you go to Neptune, leave your sunglasses at home. The Sun is 900 times dimmer when viewed from Neptune than from Earth, and it really just looks like a bright star far out in the darkness of space.

This image, taken by *Voyager 2*, was the first to show Neptune's rings in detail. The two main rings are five to ten times brighter than in previous images, which is due to the angle at which the spacecraft was positioned.

put it at −391° Fahrenheit (−235°C), the coldest of any known object in the entire solar system.

Triton is one of just two Neptune moons that can be seen from Earth with a telescope. The other moon that is visible is named Nereid, and it is far smaller than Triton, at a mere 211 miles (340 km) in diameter. Nereid completes its orbit around the planet from nearly 3.5 million miles (5.5 million km) away.

Because it's so far away, it only makes sense that it would take much longer for Nereid to make the journey around Neptune than it would for Triton. And that's exactly the case. Nereid, in a strange coincidence, orbits Neptune once every 365.21 days. That's almost exactly one Earth year, the same amount of time it takes Earth to orbit the Sun.

Neptune's other moons, discovered thanks to *Voyager 2*'s photographs, are much smaller than Triton. The smallest is only about 20 miles (32.2 km) in diameter, a distance a fast runner could cover in several hours. Think about that next time you race your friends!

The Rings of Neptune

Neptune, like the other gas planets of the solar system, is surrounded by rings. These rings, part of the planet's atmosphere, have puzzled astronomers for years. What are they made of? Are they really rings? That is, do they go all the way around the planet, or are they just incomplete arcs? Why are there rings around Neptune but not around Earth or the other non-gas planets?

For a long time, scientists were convinced that the fuzzy halos surrounding Neptune were arcs. Then *Voyager 2* arrived at the planet. The first photographs back from the spacecraft showed what appeared to be arcs, or incomplete circles, of orbiting material, things like chunks and clumps of car-sized rock and small clouds of dust. But then the astronomers looked more closely. Using computers to make the images clearer and more precise, they found these arcs were, in fact, rings. They only appeared to be arcs because the orbiting debris was so spread out that the rings were hard to see.

Using starlight as a guide, *Voyager 2*'s cameras picked up three separate rings in all. As light from the stars passed through the rings, it reflected off the millions of particles. These reflections allowed scientists on Earth to analyze Neptune's atmosphere and determine where it is thick, where it is thin, and what it is made of.

Before long, scientists had named the rings. The so-called Main Ring is, as the name implies, the major ring around Neptune. It is the biggest and outermost ring and has three areas where the orbiting rocks and dust appear much brighter (and therefore more concentrated) than elsewhere in the ring. These bright areas look like arcs and have been nicknamed Liberty, Equality, and Fraternity. The second ring is called the Diffuse Ring. Diffuse means "spread out," so this ring has far less material than the main ring does. Finally, the third ring is called the Plateau Ring. Plateaus are broad and flat, so you can guess what this ring looks like. The Plateau Ring has very few large chunks and is instead made primarily of extremely small, dustlike particles.

Neptune's Numbers

- Neptune is the fourth largest in diameter of the nine planets.

- Neptune is the eighth planet from the Sun, though it is sometimes the ninth when its orbit crosses with Pluto's.

- Neptune's atmosphere is –360°F (–218°C) because it is so far from the Sun.

- Neptune is 2.79 billion miles (4.5 billion km) from the Sun.

- Neptune's distance from Earth ranges from 4.3 billion miles (2.7 trillion km) to 2.9 trillion miles (4.6 trillion km). Neptune's average distance from the Sun is 30.06 times as far as Earth is from the Sun.

- Neptune's diameter is 30,775 miles (49,528 km). This is 3.883 times that of Earth's diameter.

- Neptune takes 60,000 days to make one complete orbit around the Sun. Compare that to Earth, which takes just 365 days. This means one year on Neptune is equivalent to 165 Earth years.

- The average speed at which Neptune orbits the Sun is 3.3 miles per second (5.43 km/s). Earth travels much faster, at 18.49 miles per second (29.78 km/s).

- Neptune, like Earth, sits at an angle on its axis. The inclination is 29.6 degrees.

- Thirteen satellites (that we know about), including eight named moons and four unnamed moons, orbit Neptune.

- One day (one full rotation on its axis) on Neptune lasts for exactly 16.11 hours. An Earth day, on the other hand, is exactly 24 hours.

- Neptune's mass is 102,430,000,000,000,000,000,000,000 kilograms. This is 17.22 times that of Earth's mass.

- Neptune's volume is 62,540,000,000,000 cubic kilometers; this is 57.74 times that of Earth's volume.

- The force of gravity on Neptune is 1.14 times that on Earth.

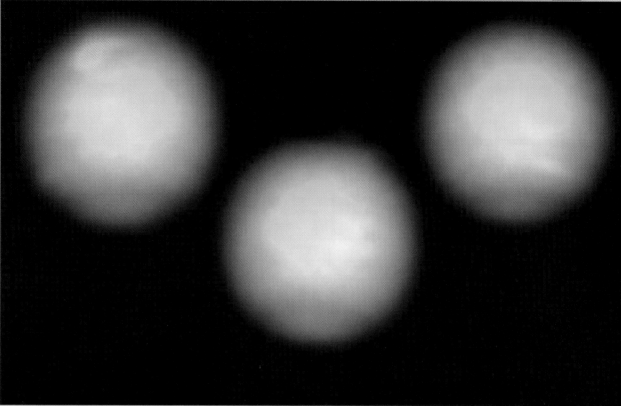

These three images of Neptune, taken by the Hubble Space Telescope, not only reveal the intense color of Neptune, but also the changing weather patterns. From left to right, the images were taken on October 10, November 2, and October 18, 1994. The pink areas reveal the planet's moving weather systems.

Neptune's Atmosphere

To put it bluntly, you'd have no chance of survival on Neptune, and that's not because the native "Neptunians" would take you away and chop you into pieces for their science experiments. In fact, there is no life on Neptune. Why? You can blame the atmosphere.

To understand Neptune's atmosphere, it might help to first take a look at Earth's atmosphere. Earth's atmosphere consists of about 78 percent nitrogen gas and 21 percent oxygen. Other gases also exist, especially carbon dioxide, but they're found in only extremely small amounts. It's this unique blend of invisible gases

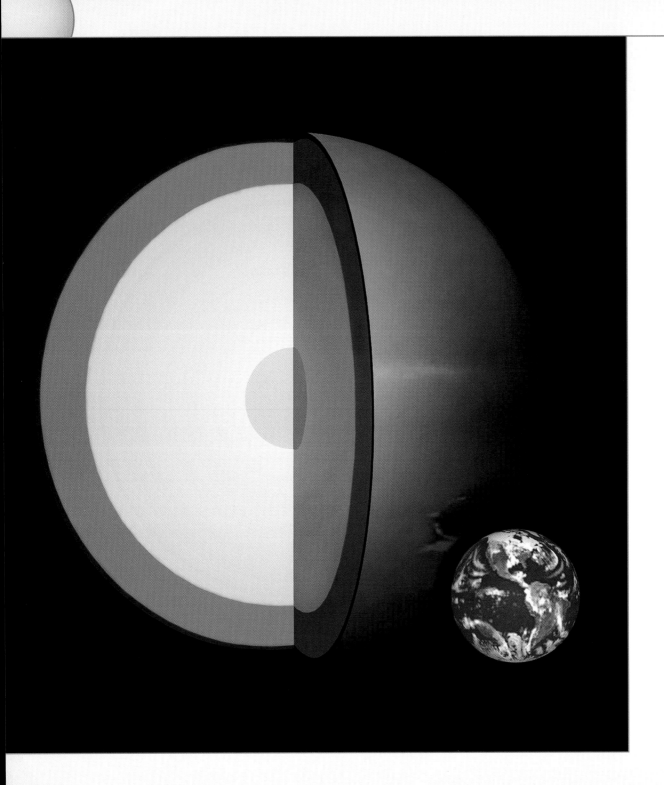

It is sometimes hard to imagine the enormity of celestial objects. We often only read the numbers and statistics. This diagram puts the size of Neptune into scale. Earth, which is at the bottom right, is shown compared to the gas giant.

that allows humans and all forms of life to breathe and trees and plants to grow.

Neptune's atmosphere, on the other hand, lacks both nitrogen and oxygen. According to the information collected from *Voyager 2* and compiled by the National Space Science Data Center (NSSDC), Neptune's atmospheric composition includes 85 percent hydrogen, 13 percent helium, and just more than 2 percent methane. There are also traces of ammonia, ethane, acetylene, carbon monoxide, and hydrogen sulfide, as well as things like ammonia ice, water ice, ammonia hydrosulfide, and methane ice.

Except for the ice, which has no chance of ever thawing out because Neptune is so cold, these ingredients are not friendly. The gases are toxic to life, or at least to life as we know it. Were you to step outside your spacecraft without your protective space suit, this poisonous concoction would kill you instantly.

If you look at Neptune from space, as *Voyager 2* did in 1989, the planet looks bluish green. This blue-green color is caused by all the methane in the atmosphere. When light strikes the methane gas, as starlight does all the time, blue wavelengths and green wavelengths of the light are reflected back, while red and other wavelengths are absorbed. This distinctive color is unique to Neptune.

What Is Neptune Made Of?

Earth is made of a hot, molten liquid core surrounded by layers upon layers of rock. On top of all that rock is earth, the soil in which trees and plants can grow. Vast oceans cover much of Earth, and mountains, valleys, plains, and many other unique features make up the rest of the landscape.

On Neptune things are a little different. Actually, they're very different. Neptune, like Earth, has a relatively small central core of melted rock, which is about the size of Earth. This core gives off intense amounts of heat, pretty much all the heat that Neptune ever gets.

Beyond the core, things start to change. The next layer out is made of very cold frozen water. Then, a little closer to the surface, the water changes to a mixture of hydrogen, helium, and methane gas. This is why Neptune is known as a gas giant. Other than its core and the water layer, Neptune is made entirely of gas. There is no solid surface like that found on Earth. It's just one giant ball of extremely toxic gas.

Three

Neptune's Violent Weather

Were there life on Neptune and should they have a television station with a real live weatherman reporting on the weather (and speaking English), this is what you might hear:

Good evening, everyone. We've got bad news once again. The weekend is not shaping up like we hoped. You might even want to stay inside for the next few days because the forecast is not good.

First off, we've got high winds ahead. Expect gusts of anywhere between 600 and 800 miles per hour (966 to 1,287 km/h). That cold spell we've been seeing is going to continue for quite some time—forever, as far as we can tell. It's going to be another long, dark day today, folks, so hunker down and enjoy your life indoors.

From here, the news would only get worse. Neptune's weather is among the worst known anywhere in the solar system. Storms can zip around the planet at thousands of miles per hour. Winds, which blow in a westerly direction, make a hurricane on Earth look like a gentle breeze. Temperatures are so cold that if you stepped outside you would freeze instantly, that is, if you somehow managed to survive breathing the poisonous gas that makes up the atmosphere. Since the sun is 900 times dimmer on Neptune than it is on Earth, darkness is the norm on this inhospitable planet.

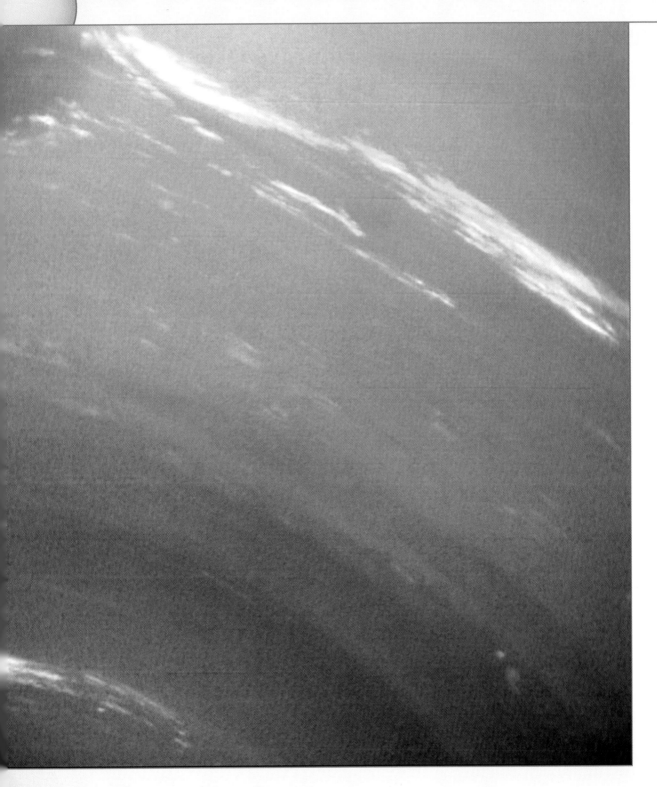

Neptune has some of the strongest winds in the solar system. This image was taken by *Voyager 2* at a distance of 370,000 miles (590,000 km). The long and thin white areas are clouds. These stretched-out clouds are evidence that Neptune has some of the strongest winds in the solar system.

Scientists have been baffled by Neptune's weather ever since *Voyager 2*'s photographs showed images of the Great Dark Spot revolving around the planet. This giant cloud was a massive storm system surrounded by vast white clouds of frozen methane and was bigger than Earth itself. The Great Dark Spot was no ordinary storm system. Zipping around Neptune's southern hemisphere, the storm's winds hit speeds of up to 1,490 miles per hour (2,400 km/h). These winds were and still are the fastest recorded in the entire solar system.

Today, in a weird twist of science that has yet to be explained, the Great Dark Spot has disappeared from astronomers' radar screens. When the Hubble Space Telescope took pictures of Neptune in 1994, the spot was nowhere to be found. No one knows for sure where it has gone, but scientists do have their theories. Some think the spot is concealed behind other parts of the atmosphere. Maybe the storm ducked under a thick layer of gas. Others suggest that the storm blew itself out. Like storms on Earth, they say, it was only a matter of time before the Great Dark Spot ran out of steam.

However, there is good news for Neptune weather buffs. Although the original Great Dark Spot is still missing, a new one has been discovered. Hubble images have located a second storm system that appears to be very similar to the first, only this time it's cruising around the planet's northern hemisphere. Scientists are in the process of studying this spot.

Other storm systems have also come and gone. One, nicknamed DS2, was nabbed on camera by *Voyager 2* and has since disappeared. Others have had similar fates. You might think scientists would become frustrated by constantly losing track of the storms they find on this distant planet, but they don't. Instead, they've used what they've learned and come to the conclusion that Neptune's atmosphere and weather are always on the go. Like those here on Earth, the planet's weather

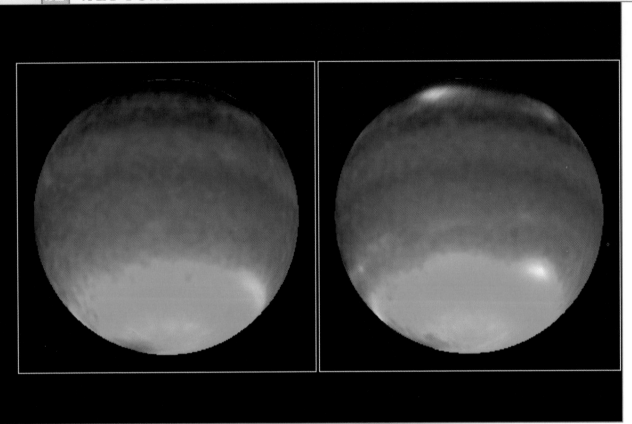

These two images of Neptune were taken by the Hubble Space Telescope on August 13, 1996. They show opposite sides of the planet. The areas in white are clouds. The highest clouds, which are at the top of the right-hand image, appear in yellow and red. In the dark blue belt just below the equator, winds are blowing at nearly 900 miles per hour (1,448 km/h).

systems are on the move. They change all the time. The main difference is the baseline from which Neptune's weather emerges. In one particular region on Earth, things might be totally calm for a week before a raging storm appears, but the weather on Neptune is always bad. When Great Dark Spots or DS2s appear, the weather just gets worse.

Science and the Weather

The causes of Neptune's weather are a complete mystery to scientists. The wind is maddening. The temperature is freezing. And the Sun is practically nonexistent.

It's this last point about the Sun that baffles scientists the most. What, they wonder, drives Neptune's horrendous weather if the Sun does not? On Earth, the Sun plays an important role in the creation of weather systems. The Sun heats Earth and its oceans, causing warm air and moisture to rise from Earth's surface into the atmosphere. When the warm air collides with colder air high off the ground, winds are created and storms are formed.

On Neptune, with sunlight hundreds of times dimmer than here on Earth, things must work differently, but scientists still can't put a handle on it. But that's not for lack of trying. Astronomers have been using Hubble photographs combined with images taken from NASA's Infrared Telescope Facility on the extinct volcano Mauna Kea in Hawaii to study weather patterns on Neptune. The high-powered telescopes are providing some of the best pictures of Neptune's weather ever seen.

Once thing scientists have learned is that Neptune's high winds blow in a westward direction, opposite of the planet's eastward

The Farthest Planet from the Sun . . . Sometimes

Neptune is widely considered to be the eighth most distant planet from the Sun, located between Uranus, which is number seven, and Pluto, which is number nine. Pluto, however, has such a long, elliptical orbit that, every once in a while, its path dips inside Neptune's. When that happens, as was the case between 1979 and 1999, Neptune becomes the ninth and farthest planet from the Sun, and Pluto takes the eighth spot. So next time you hear people say Pluto is the most distant planet in the entire solar system, tell them they'd better check their calendars to make sure. They might want to reconsider.

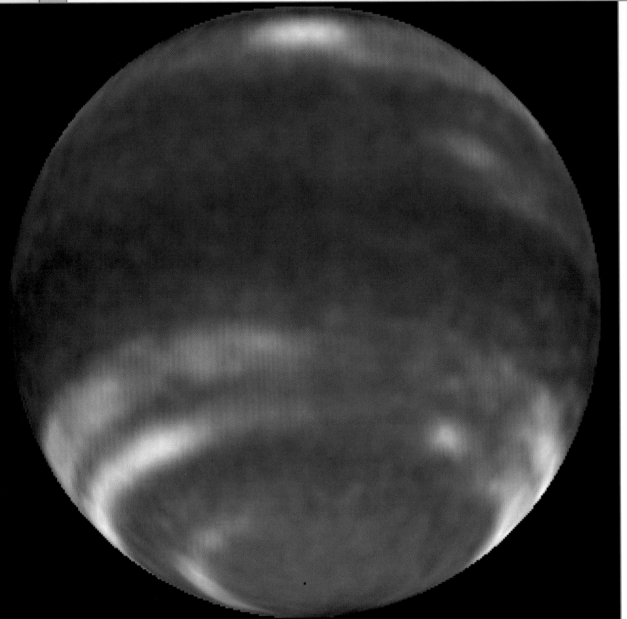

This image of Neptune, taken by the Hubble Space Telescope in 2002, shows springtime on the planet. Scientists can detect the seasonal change because the clouds in the southern hemisphere appear wider and brighter. This change is probably due to the increase in sunlight, similar to what happens on Earth.

direction of rotation. They've also learned that Neptune's clouds form in layers, like they do on Earth. Some clouds are extremely high, while others seem to hover just over the planet's gaseous surface. Most significant, perhaps, is the finding that bands of weather are formed in line with Neptune's equator, the imaginary line that divides the planet into northern and southern hemispheres. A similar phenomenon occurs in Earth's equatorial region.

So why are scientists so interested in Neptune's weather? One reason is simple: because it's strange. There's always something to learn from the unknown, something to gain from solving seemingly unsolvable problems. Should scientists unravel the mystery of Neptune's weather, there's no telling what might come next.

The Present and the Future

With all this talk about Neptune, there's one obvious question that has yet to be asked: Will humans ever live there? The answer is easy: no way. Neptune just won't allow it. The environment is too hostile for human life. If humans ever colonize a planet other than Earth, it won't be Neptune. We might colonize Mars, because it is similar to Earth, but not Neptune.

With that settled, what's Neptune got in store for us over the next few hundred years? Well, for one, Neptune will continue, as it has for billions of years, to orbit the Sun as one of the nine planets in our solar system. And as it does, scientists will continue to train their telescopes to the sky and study every last detail of its motion.

Using data they collect on Neptune and other planets, they'll learn more about how objects in space influence each other. They'll probably try to determine Neptune's ultimate fate: Will it burn out one day when it comes too close to the Sun? Will it collide with another massive object in space and explode into trillions of pieces? Will its hot core cool down, causing it to change shape or speed or size? Or will it just continue on its same path forever?

NASA is working to solve many of the mysteries of space, and Neptune is just one of them. Each year, with each new launch of a space shuttle with high-tech experiments and with each new million-dollar telescope designed to look just a bit deeper into space, progress is made.

A Pinprick of Light

It's really hard to see Neptune from Earth, but if you have a pair of binoculars (or better yet, a telescope) you might be able to find it in your sights. The planet can be found in the southern horizon and will appear to be little more than a pinprick of light. It's so small, in fact, that you'll probably need a map of the skies to find it.

The Internet is a good source for sky maps, which are charts of the stars and their relative locations in space. Jump online and see what you can find, then wait for a dark night to take a look.

Neptunium

The ninety-third element of the periodic table is neptunium. This radioactive metal was named after the planet Neptune because the element before it is uranium, named after Uranus. Since Neptune is the next planet out after Uranus, it only made sense to call the next element neptunium. Can you guess what the element plutonium is named after?

Edwin McMillan (1907–1991), shown here, was an American physicist who discovered neptunium.

Much of what we know now about Neptune has been taken from the data collected by just one spacecraft: *Voyager 2,* the only spacecraft to ever visit the planet. Should scientists determine that they need more information, they'll surely send more—perhaps *Voyager 3* or *Voyager 4.* Maybe, if technology allows it, that spacecraft will hold an astronaut. And maybe, if you're up to the challenge, that astronaut will be you.

1613: The famous Italian astronomer and physicist Galileo Galilei sees Neptune for the first time but mistakes it for a star.

1820: Alexis Bouvard discovers that the orbit of Uranus, the neighboring planet to soon-to-be-discovered Neptune, is slightly different than had been calculated. This suggests that the gravity of another body must have been influencing the orbit of Uranus.

1846: Johann Gottfried Galle, an employee of the Berlin Observatory, discovers the planet with his telescope. The object is the size of a pinprick and is almost exactly where Urbain-Jean-Joseph LeVerrier suggested it should be.

John Couch Adams discovers Neptune independently of Johann Gottfried Galle around the same time, possibly even before.

The first of Neptune's moons to be discovered, Triton, is spotted by the English scientist William Lassell.

1977: *Voyager 2* launches. It is scheduled to explore Jupiter and Saturn and then continue to Uranus and Neptune.

1989: *Voyager 2* arrives at Neptune. It takes photographs of Neptune, discovering the Great Dark Spot. *Voyager 2* also discovers six new moons and that Triton possesses geysers similar to those found on Earth.

2003: The International Astronomical Union announces on September 3 the discovery by Hubble of a new satellite orbiting Neptune.

Glossary

astronaut A person trained to travel to space in a spacecraft.

astronomer A scientist who studies space.

atmosphere The mixture of gases that surrounds a planet.

celestial Of or relating to the sky.

colonize To move to and establish a settlement in.

data Information collected as part of a scientific study.

density The amount of matter in a given amount of space.

diameter The distance through the center of an object from one end to the other.

equator A circular band that divides a planet into its two hemispheres.

gas giant Any of the planets that are composed mostly or entirely of gas.

geologic Relating to the study of the solid matter of a celestial body.

geyser A spring that spews liquid from beneath the surface of a celestial body.

gravity The force of attraction that occurs between two bodies in space.

hemisphere Half of a celestial sphere.

interplanetary The space between planets.

mass The amount of matter in an object, which determines its weight.

neptunium The element in the periodic table that was named after Neptune.

observatory A housing for a telescope where celestial bodies can be observed.

orbit The path a planet or other object in space takes as it revolves around something else.

phenomenon A spectacular occurrence or incident.

revolve To travel around an object following a particular orbit.

satellite A relatively small object that orbits another larger object.

solar system The region of space including the Sun and the nine planets and other objects that orbit the Sun.

spacecraft A vehicle used to travel through and study space and celestial objects.

theoretical What is believed to be true but cannot be proven.

uranium The element in the periodic table that was named after Uranus.

volume The amount of space that an object occupies.

Adler Planetarium & Astronomy Museum
1300 South Lake Shore Drive
Chicago, IL 60605-2403
(312) 922-STAR
Web site: http://www.adlerplanetarium.org

Hayden Planetarium
American Museum of Natural History
Central Park West at 79th Street
New York, NY 10024
(212) 769-5913
Web site: http://www.haydenplanetarium.org

Jet Propulsion Laboratory
1200 East California Boulevard
Pasadena, CA 91125
(626) 395-6811
Web site: http://www.jpl.nasa.gov

National Aeronautics and Space Administration (NASA)
Headquarters Information Center
Washington, DC 20546-0001
(202) 358-0000
Web site: http://www.nasa.gov

Smithsonian National Air and Space Museum
Seventh Street and Independence Avenue SW
Washington, DC 20560
(202) 357-2700
Web site: http://www.nasm.si.edu

Space Telescope Science Institute
3700 San Martin Drive
Johns Hopkins University Homewood Campus
Baltimore, MD 21218
(410) 338-4700
Web site: http://www.stsci.edu/resources

Web Sites

Due to the changing nature of Internet links, the Rosen Publishing Group, Inc., has developed an online list of Web sites related to the subject of this book. This site is updated regularly. Please use this link to access the list:

http://www.rosenlinks.com/lnp/nept

For Further Reading

Cole, Michael D. *Neptune: The Eighth Planet* (Countdown to Space). Berkeley Heights, NJ: Enslow Publishers, Inc., 2002.

Hunt, Garry E., and Patrick Moore. *Atlas of Neptune.* Cambridge, England: Cambridge University Press, 1994.

Littmann, Mark. *Planets Beyond: Discovering the Outer Solar System.* New York: John Wiley and Sons, 1988.

Miner, Ellis D., and Randii R. Wessen. *Neptune: The Planet, Rings, and Satellites.* London: Praxis Press, 2002.

Tabak, John. *A Look at Neptune.* New York: Franklin Watts, Inc., 2003.

Bibliography

NASA Jet Propulsion Laboratory Web Site. "Voyager: The Grandest Tour." Retrieved August 5, 2003 (http://www.jpl.nasa.gov/voyager).

NASA National Space Science Data Center Web Site. "Neptune." Retrieved August 5, 2003 (http://nssdc.gsfc.nasa.gov/planetary/planets/neptunepage.html).

NASA Solar System Exploration Web Site. "Neptune." Retrieved August 8, 2003 (http://solarsystem.nasa.gov/features/planets/neptune/neptune.html).

The Nine Planets Web Site. "A Multimedia Tour of the Solar System." Retrieved August 23, 2003 (http://www.nineplanets.org).

Smithsonian National Air and Space Museum Web Site. Retrieved August 15, 2003 (http://www.nasm.si.edu).

Solar Views Web Site. "Neptune." Retrieved August 22, 2003 (http://www.solarviews.com/eng/neptune.htm).

Index

A

Adams, John Couch, 11, 18–19

B

Berlin Observatory, 10
Bouvard, Alexis, 7–9, 10

D

Diffuse Ring, 23
DS2, 31, 32

E

Earth, 5, 6, 7, 8, 14, 15, 21, 23, 34,
    35, 36, 37
atmosphere of, 18, 25–27, 28
orbit of, 9, 22
surface of, 27, 28, 33
weather systems on, 29, 31, 32, 33

G

Galilei, Galileo, 11
Galle, Johann Gottfried, 10
geysers, 14, 21
Great Dark Spot, 15–17, 31, 32

H

helium, 6, 27, 28
Hubble Space Telescope, 31, 33
hydrogen, 6, 27, 28

I

International Space Station, 6

J

Jupiter, 12, 14

L

Laplace, Pierre-Simon, 7

Lassell, William, 18–19
LeVerrier, Urbain-Jean-Joseph,
    10, 11

M

Main Ring, 23
Mars, 6, 36
methane, 6, 21, 27, 28, 31
Moon, the, 5, 6, 9, 14, 19

N

National Aeronautics and Space
    Administration (NASA), 6, 12, 14,
    33, 36
National Space Science Data Center
    (NSSDC), 27
Neptune
    atmosphere of, 6, 15, 18, 21, 22,
        23, 25–27, 31
    composition of, 27–28
    discovery of, 6, 10–11
    exploration of, 12–17, 23, 31, 33,
        36, 38
    moons of, 6, 18–22
    orbit of, 24, 36
    rings of, 14–15, 22–23
    size of, 6, 24
    temperatures on, 15, 24, 29, 32
    weather of, 15, 17, 18, 29–35
    winds on, 17, 29, 31, 32, 33–34
neptunium, 38
Nereid, 22
nitrogen, 21, 27

O

oxygen, 25, 27

P

Paris Observatory, 10

Plateau Ring, 23
Pluto, 33

S

Saturn, 12, 14
Scooter, 17
Sedna, 6
solar system, 5, 6, 7, 12, 18, 19, 22,
    29, 31, 33, 36
Sun, the, 5, 6, 7, 22, 29, 32,
    33, 36

T

Triton, 14, 18–22

U

Uranus, 7–9, 12, 14, 33, 38

V

Voyager missions, 12–15
Voyager 1, 12–14
Voyager 2, 12–14, 15, 21, 22, 23, 27,
    31, 38

About the Author

Chris Hayhurst is a writer living in Colorado.

Credits

Cover, pp 4–5, 20, 21, 22, 30 NASA/JPL/CalTech; pp. 8, 26 © Mark Garlick/Science Photo Library/Photo Researchers, Inc.; pp. 10, 12, 38 © Science Photo Library/Photo Researchers, Inc.; p. 13 © NASA/Kennedy Space Center; p. 15 © Roger Ressmeyer/Corbis; pp. 16, 19 © NASA/NSSDC; p. 25 NASA/JPL/H. Hammel/MIT; pp. 32, 34 NASA/L. Sromovsky and P. Fry (University of Wisconsin–Madison); p. 37 © Time Life Pictures/Getty Images, Inc.

Designer: Thomas Forget; Editor: Nicholas Croce

COMSEWOGUE PUBLIC LIBRARY
170 TERRYVILLE ROAD
PORT JEFFERSON STATION
NEW YORK 11776